My Best Book of Weather

Simon Adams

KING*f*ISHER

Contents

Created for Kingfisher Publications Plc
by Picthall & Gunzi Limited

Author: Simon Adams
Consultant: Ron Lobeck
Editor: Lauren Robertson
Designer: Floyd Sayers
Illustrators: Mike Saunders,
  Roger Stewart

KINGFISHER
Kingfisher Publications Plc,
New Penderel House,
283–288 High Holborn,
London WC1V 7HZ
www.kingfisherpub.com

First published by Kingfisher
Publications Plc 2001

10 9 8 7 6 5 4 3 2 1

1TR/0401/WKT/MAR(MAR)/128KMA

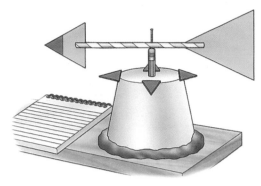

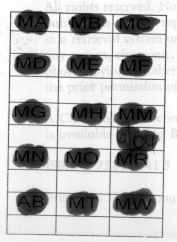

What is weather?

Satellite

Exosphere
This layer lies 700–800km from Earth. It is made up of thin gases that drift off into space. This is where satellites orbit our planet.

Space shuttle

Thermosphere
This layer lies 80–700km from Earth. It is the hottest part of the atmosphere, where aurora lights appear and meteorites burn out.

Aurora lights

Shooting stars

Mesosphere
The mesosphere is 50–80km from Earth and is the coldest part of the atmosphere.

Weather balloon

Stratosphere
This layer is 12–50km above the ground. Aeroplanes fly in the thin air of the stratosphere.

Aeroplane

Troposphere
The troposphere is up to 12km above the ground and this is where all our weather happens.

Clouds

Earth is wrapped in a thick layer of air called the atmosphere. This air is made up of gases and it can be hot or cold, wet or dry, and can move fast or stay still. The changes in the air closest to Earth are known as the weather. The Sun's rays keep our bodies warm. Clouds keep us cool by day and warm at night. Winds blow the clouds around the sky. And rain helps plants to grow, and fills our rivers and lakes.

The atmosphere

High above Earth, the atmosphere stretches 800km into space. Scientists have divided it into five invisible layers. These layers are made up of a mixture of gases, such as oxygen and nitrogen. We use satellites in the highest layer to take pictures of the weather from above. Experts on the ground can then tell us what the weather will be like in the next few days or weeks.

A weather satellite takes photographs of the weather from space.

Cloud formations are easy to see from space.

How weather is made

The weather is created by a mixture of water, heat and air. The Sun heats up the air, which makes it move. This moving air is called wind, and it carries heat and water vapour, which is an invisible gas. Clouds, rain, snow and fog are made from water vapour.

Walkers stand on a hillside watching the weather change

Weather and us

The weather affects our daily lives, so we are told by scientists what it will be like in the days ahead. This is called weather forecasting. The study of the weather is called meteorology, and the scientists who do this are called meteorologists. They use temperature, wind speed, air pressure measurements and satellite photographs to forecast the weather.

Light helium gas lifts a weather balloon high into the atmosphere so the instruments it carries can record the weather

Cameras in weather satellites take pictures of weather formations

Watching the weather

Weather stations on land and at sea, aeroplanes, weather balloons and satellites in space are all used for watching and measuring weather. They help scientists to make a weather forecast.

A thermometer measures temperature

An anemometer records wind speed

Weather aeroplanes are used for watching the weather from the sky

A barograph - a type of barometer - keeps a record of changes in air pressure

Weather maps show weather formations

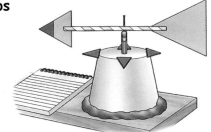

A weather vane shows wind direction

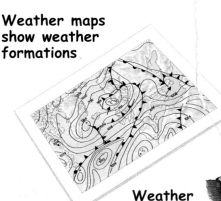

Weather stations at sea record changes

Weather power

The weather can be used to make energy that does not cause pollution. Heat from the Sun can drive a car or warm a house. Wind power turns wind turbines to pump water. Without the weather, we could use only oil, coal and gas for our power, and these fuels may run out.

Solar panels on a house use heat from the Sun to heat water and provide warmth

Giant wind turbines produce electricity

Panels on solar-powered cars change sunlight into electricity which is used to drive the car

Studying the weather

The speed of the wind, the temperature of the air, and the amount of rainfall can all be measured using simple equipment. You can note down what type of weather happens at the same time each day, and see how the weather changes over time.

School students studying the weather

Weather through the ages

Earth's weather is always changing, and these changes affect all living things on Earth. Thousands of years ago, cold periods called ice ages or glacials covered the Earth with ice. Warm periods, called interglacials, turned parts of the planet into desert. Today, we are living in an interglacial period.

The dinosaurs may have died out because they could not breathe when volcanic dust filled the air

Weather and extinction

Some types of animals and plants can survive when the weather changes suddenly, but others die out, or become extinct. Scientists believe that the dinosaurs were killed by a sudden change in the weather millions of years ago. Some think that the dust from an erupting volcano filled the sky and turned the Earth dark and cold. Others believe that the dust was caused by a meteorite hitting Earth.

Woolly rhinoceros

Sometimes scientists travel to the coldest places on Earth to carry out research on the weather

Meteorologists use special equipment to core the ice for samples

Discovering the past

Scientists can discover what the weather was like in the past by looking at samples of ice, rock and earth. Ice that is buried in ice caps and glaciers shows the weather conditions at the time that the ice was created, even if it was formed thousands of years ago.

Ice age world

Ten thousand years ago, Earth was much colder than it is today and looked quite different. Large sheets of ice covered one third of the planet. Mammoths and other animals that lived at that time were covered with thick hair to keep out the cold.

Many areas of land on Earth were covered with ice during the recent ice age

Reindeer

Woolly mammoths

9

Climate and seasons

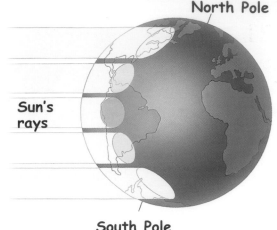

The usual weather pattern in a country is called its climate. Different areas of the planet have different climates – some places are mostly hot or cold, and others are usually wet or dry. The weather changes throughout the year, and these changes are known as the seasons. Most places have four seasons, but some have only two.

North Pole

Sun's rays

South Pole

Hottest and coldest

The climate is hottest at the Equator and coldest at the North and South Poles. This is because more of the Sun's rays reach Earth at the Equator than at the Poles. In the mountains and by the sea, the climate is cold. Away from the coasts, it is often hotter and drier by day, but colder at night.

Life at the South Pole is cold and icy

A tropical rainforest is warm and wet

Many desert areas are hot and dry

Different climates

The polar climate – at the North and South Poles – is very cold. Near the Equator, the climate is hot and is described as tropical or Equatorial. In between the Poles and the Equator is the temperate zone. This is either warm or cool, depending on the time of year.

The changing seasons

Seasons change during the year. When it is winter in the northern part of Earth, or northern hemisphere, it is summer in the southern part, or southern hemisphere.

Spring

Spring is the season when the days grow longer and warmer. Nights are cold and the weather may change frequently.

Summer

Summer is the hottest season of the year. The Sun is high in the sky, the days are long and there may be thunderstorms.

Autumn

The nights get longer and the days shorter in autumn. The temperature cools down. It is often misty and the ground may be frosty.

Winter

Winter is the coldest season of the year. The Sun is low in the sky and the days are short. Snow can fall and ice form in the cold nights.

Monsoon winds bring heavy rain that floods parts of Asia

Wet and dry seasons

In East Africa, India and South East Asia, there are only two seasons – the wet season and the dry season. In the wet season, the air is humid and monsoon winds blow in from the sea, carrying heavy rain. In the dry season, monsoon winds blow cool, dry air from the land out to sea.

The power of the Sun

Life on Earth would not exist without the Sun's warmth and light. As Earth spins every day on its axis, the side that faces the Sun warms up in the daylight. The side that is hidden from the Sun cools down in the darkness. The change in temperature causes winds to blow, clouds to form, and all other types of weather, such as snow and rain, to develop. It can also lead to floods or droughts.

Too much Sun

People enjoy playing in the Sun and sunbathing in hot weather. But harmful rays from the Sun can burn the skin and cause skin diseases.

Huge clouds form in the Sun's heat, and hurricanes, cyclones and typhoons flare up in the tropics.

Winds from the west, called westerlies, blow on either side of the tropics.

Clouds around the Equator show that Earth's winds meet in this area.

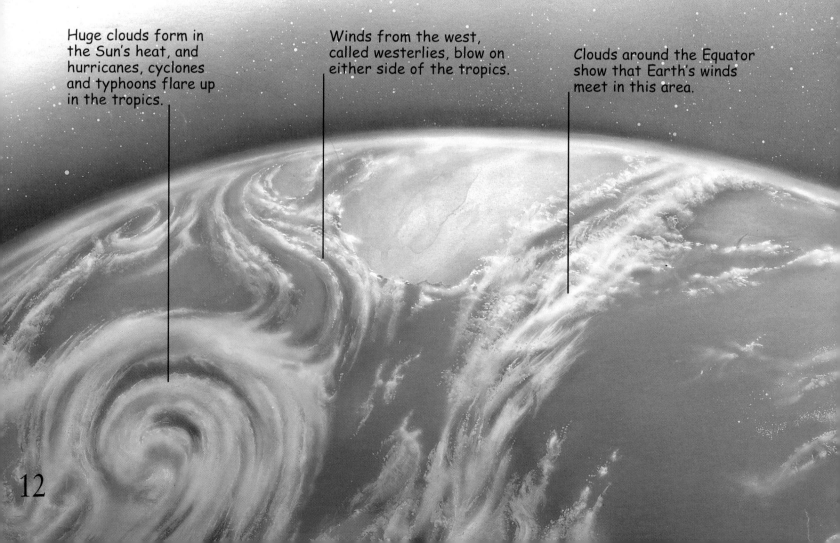

12

Sun energy

The Sun affects all our weather. Its heat makes water evaporate, or change into a gas, to form water vapour. The heat also makes the water vapour rise and form clouds. In the tropics, the heat of the Sun stirs up moist sea air and creates storm clouds. The Sun also makes the wind blow by heating the air and changing its temperature and pressure.

The Sun's rays travel to Earth 150 million km away

The Sun's heat makes water from the ocean evaporate and form clouds.

The Earth from space

Drought

Many hot parts of the planet have long periods with no rain, and this can cause droughts. The heat makes rivers dry up and kills plants. Cracks appear on the land and crops cannot grow, so people do not have enough food to eat.

When the wind blows

Air presses down on us all the time. Cold, heavy air sinks and creates high pressure. The heavy air warms up and keeps the weather fine. Warm air is light, so it rises and creates low pressure. As it rises, new air blows in to take its place. This is called wind. The weather in low pressure conditions is usually wet and windy. Winds can be soft and gentle, or fast and strong.

Beaufort Scale

The Beaufort Scale was invented by an English admiral, Sir Francis Beaufort. The scale measures how strong the wind is, from force 0 to 12.

1 In forces 0–3, there is no wind or only a light breeze. Clouds drift slowly and the sea is flat or calm.

2 In forces 4–7, the wind is stronger. Trees sway in the breeze and the sea is choppy with waves.

3 In forces 8–12, the wind is fast and powerful. The sea is rough with big waves.

The Coriolis effect

Earth spins on its axis like a top, so the air that moves across the planet flows in a curve. This is called the Coriolis effect. Air moving from the Poles to the Equator curves to the west. Air moving from the Equator to the Poles curves to the east.

Sails full of wind

Many people enjoy sailing in a yacht or dinghy. The wind blows the sails and drives the boat forward. Sailing boats also have engines so that they can move when there is no wind.

Earth spins in this direction.

North Pole

Equator

South Pole

Winds curve to the west from the North and South Poles.

Winds blowing from the east over oceans are called 'trade winds'.

Wind makes waves form on the sea

A world of water

The air is full of water vapour gas that has evaporated from the seas and lakes. As the water vapour cools, it forms droplets of liquid water. These droplets join together and float in the air as clouds. As the water droplets get bigger, they can form huge, dark rain clouds that become heavier. They then fall to Earth as raindrops. Clouds disappear after it has rained because all the water in them has fallen to Earth.

The water cycle

Air can soak up and let go of water like a sponge. This means that the water on Earth is always being recycled. The Sun's rays heat seawater and it evaporates to become clouds. These clouds then release raindrops. The rainwater drains back to the sea along streams and rivers to begin the water cycle again.

Vapour cools and forms clouds.

Seawater evaporates in the Sun's heat.

Rainwater flows back to the sea along rivers.

Types of rain

Rain is drops of water falling to the ground from clouds. Small drops are known as drizzle. Larger raindrops fall in showers, and a heavy fall of rain is called a downpour.

Drizzle is small drops of rain falling in a soft spray. There is often drizzle when it is foggy.

A short fall of rain is called a shower. After a shower, the sky clears up and the Sun shines again.

A downpour is a heavy fall of rain. The sky is full of dark rain clouds, and puddles form.

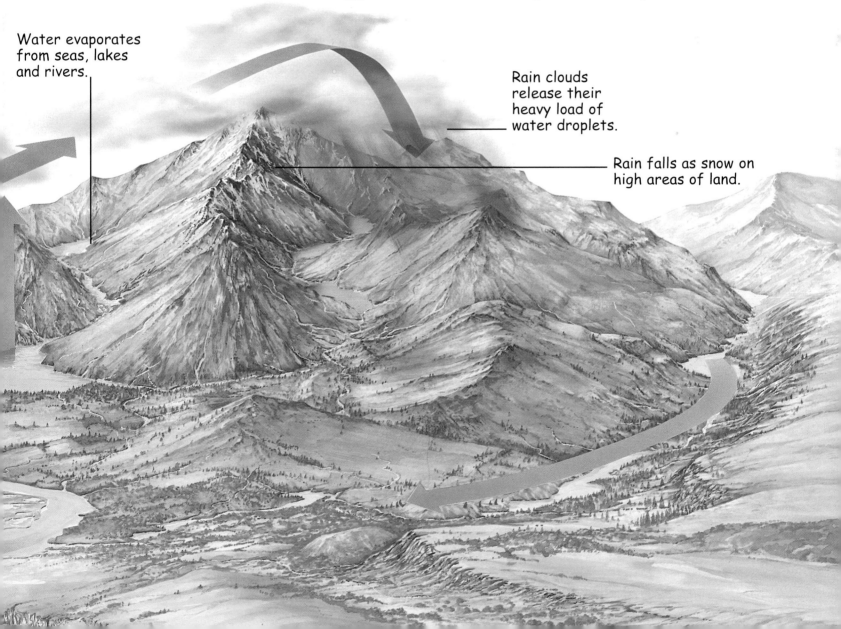

Water evaporates from seas, lakes and rivers.

Rain clouds release their heavy load of water droplets.

Rain falls as snow on high areas of land.

Cloud cover

Clouds come in many shapes and sizes. Some clouds are layered and look like the scales on a fish. Other clouds look like giant cotton wool balls in the sky. Some types of cloud can be found close to the ground as fog or mist. Highest in the sky are the cirrus clouds, which are made up of tiny ice crystals. The powerful cumulonimbus clouds are the largest. They tower above all the others, forming an icy wedge on the troposphere.

Cirrus
(10km–12km above ground)
The highest clouds in the sky are formed from ice crystals where the air is cold. Strong winds blow these clouds into wispy tails. They show that the weather is unsettled.

Altocumulus
(5–7km above ground)
These small, fluffy clouds can look like flattened balls of cotton wool that are linked together.

Nimbostratus
(0–1km above ground)
These thick, dark layers of rain cloud form close to the ground. They can bring long periods of heavy rain or snow.

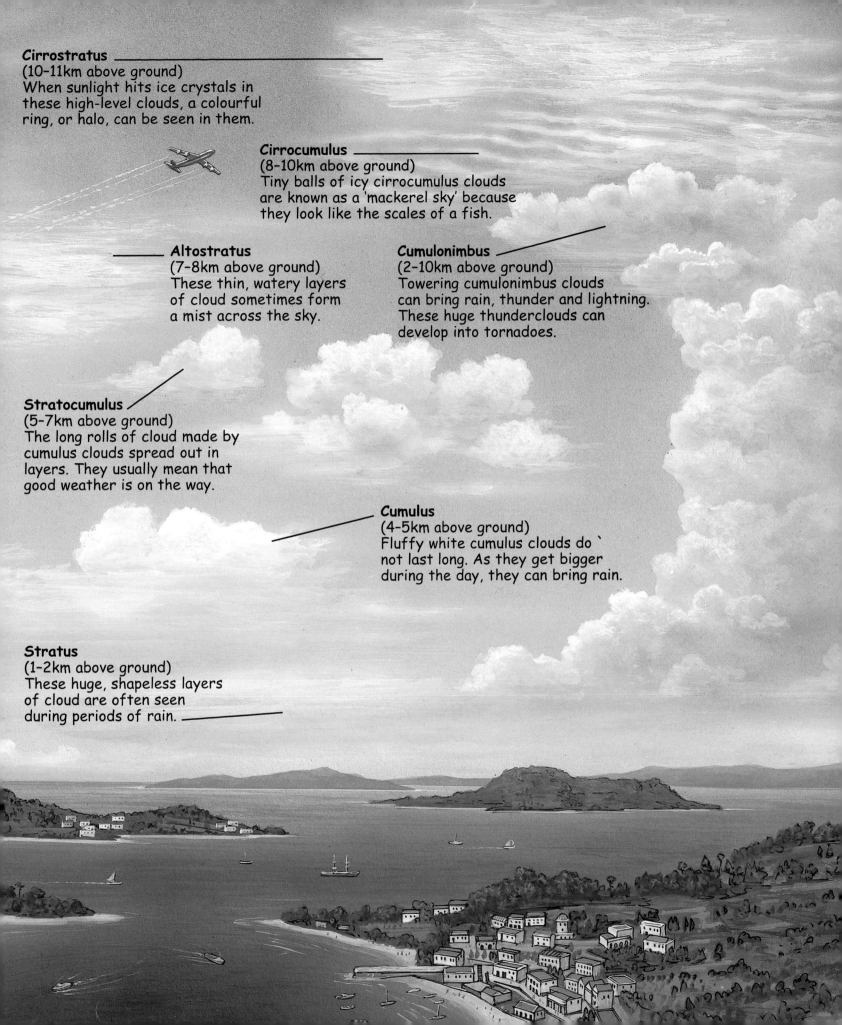

Cirrostratus
(10–11km above ground)
When sunlight hits ice crystals in these high-level clouds, a colourful ring, or halo, can be seen in them.

Cirrocumulus
(8–10km above ground)
Tiny balls of icy cirrocumulus clouds are known as a 'mackerel sky' because they look like the scales of a fish.

Altostratus
(7–8km above ground)
These thin, watery layers of cloud sometimes form a mist across the sky.

Cumulonimbus
(2–10km above ground)
Towering cumulonimbus clouds can bring rain, thunder and lightning. These huge thunderclouds can develop into tornadoes.

Stratocumulus
(5–7km above ground)
The long rolls of cloud made by cumulus clouds spread out in layers. They usually mean that good weather is on the way.

Cumulus
(4-5km above ground)
Fluffy white cumulus clouds do not last long. As they get bigger during the day, they can bring rain.

Stratus
(1–2km above ground)
These huge, shapeless layers of cloud are often seen during periods of rain.

Electric skies

Electrical thunderstorms are often exciting but can also be scary. Loud rolls of thunder can be heard many kilometres away from the heart of the storm. Lightning flashes explode from the clouds and light up a dark sky. Fork lightning is filled with electricity that is created in huge, black cumulonimbus clouds. This electricity flows down to Earth, sometimes damaging buildings and trees. Heavy rainfall or hailstones usually add to the drama.

Tree struck by lightning

How distant is a storm?

We can tell how far away a storm is by counting the seconds between the flash of lightning and the clap of thunder. Three seconds equals one kilometre.

When lightning strikes

Lightning is electrical energy, so it is hot and powerful. Its power lasts only for a few millionths of a second, but it is enough to blow a tree apart or topple a tall chimney.

20

The power of lightning

A thunderstorm can be violent and buildings are often hit by lightning. Many buildings have metal strips, called lightning conductors, inside them. These lead the electricity from the lightning safely down to Earth.

All fogged up

Fog is a cloud that forms on the ground. It looks like smoke, but it is actually tiny drops of water that hang in the air. When it is foggy, it is difficult to see things around you, and driving can be dangerous. A thick fog can stop aeroplanes from taking off and landing. Most forms of transport have to travel very slowly in a fog.

Smog in the city

A thick fog mixed with car exhaust fumes and chimney smoke is called 'smog'. Most cities have smog and the pollution can make people ill. Many countries are trying to reduce the amount of smog, by banning the use of coal fires in the home, for example.

In thick fog, boats cannot be seen, so they use lights or fog horns to warn other boats that they are on the water

A misty morning

Early morning fog on the ground is called mist. It forms after a cool, calm night. When the Sun heats up the air, the mist clears away. After cold nights, tiny drops of water can form on cold blades of grass. This is called dew.

Early morning mist on a meadow

Fogging up the river

Air is full of water vapour. When warm air cools, the water vapour forms a cloud of water droplets. If this happens near the ground, fog or mist is formed. Fog often forms over cold seas, rivers and lakes, as it has on this river in South East Asia.

Fun in the snow

Snow forms high inside clouds when the temperature is low. It is made of tiny crystals of ice. Raindrops often start to fall as ice crystals, but melt on the way down to Earth. In cold weather, ice crystals reach the ground as snowflakes. A heavy snowfall covers the ground like a thick, white blanket. Frost and ice also form when the weather is very cold.

Snow magic

Snowflakes appear to be round and white as they fall. But each one is actually a beautiful ice crystal with six sides. Like people, no two ice crystals are the same.

Icicles form on roofs

Ice rinks are made of ice that is hard and slippery enough to skate on

Snowmen and snowballs are made of wet snow that has stuck together

24

Ice crystals

In warm weather, the snow on the top of a mountain can melt and tumble down as an avalanche

Snow-packed slopes are perfect for ski-ing

Packed snow is smooth and slippery enough for sledging

Frosty windows

When the weather is very cold, water vapour in the air freezes into different types of frost. Frost can form thick ice on the ground or it can make patterns on glass (right).

25

The wildest weather

Eye in the centre of the storm

Clockwise direction of a cyclone

Typhoons, hurricanes and cyclones spiral anti-clockwise in the Northern Hemisphere and clockwise in the Southern Hemisphere

When thunderstorms happen near the Equator, they can be wild and dangerous. Sometimes storms build up over warm, tropical seas and join together to form hurricanes. These storms are also called typhoons, or tropical cyclones. Hurricane winds reach speeds of up to 360km per hour. Some of these storms can be 800km wide and 15km high. They create huge waves out at sea that flood the land.

Twisters

Huge pillars of spiralling air sometimes form beneath thunderclouds. These are called twisters, or tornadoes. Low air pressure inside the twister acts like a giant vacuum cleaner, and sucks up the air around it – as well as anything that it passes over. The winds spinning inside a twister can move at speeds of up to 400km per hour.

Tropical storms

A hurricane, typhoon or cyclone is a violent storm. These storms are made up of a spiral of fast-moving wind around a calm centre called the 'eye'. The storm brings heavy rain as well as strong winds. When hurricanes hit the land, buildings are destroyed, trees are uprooted and people can lose their lives.

Palm trees bend easily in the wind so they do not often break or become uprooted

Spectacular skies

For most of us, the weather does not change much from day to day. Some days are bright and sunny and some are cloudy or rainy. But our skies can surprise us. Rainbows appear after rain and, in certain parts of the world, the night sky can light up with coloured lights called auroras. During a violent thunderstorm, large lumps of ice may crash down to Earth from the sky. These can damage crops, dent cars and break windows.

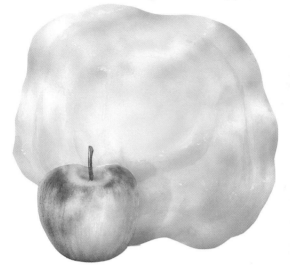

Raining ice

A hailstone is a lump of solid ice made inside a thundercloud. As it moves around in the cloud, it collects water droplets, which then freeze. The hailstone grows heavy and drops to Earth. Most hailstones are about 1cm across.

Colours in the sky

In the Arctic and Antarctic regions, the Sun's rays sometimes meet gases in the thermosphere, and we see a colourful light show in the sky. Bands of red, green and yellow lights fill the night. These are known as the aurora borealis (northern lights) in the northern hemisphere, and the aurora australis (southern lights) in the southern hemisphere.

Rainbows

A rainbow is caused by sunlight passing through millions of raindrops in the sky. As rays of light pass through the water droplets, they are broken up into seven colours – red, orange, yellow, green, blue, indigo and violet. The colours are always the same and appear in the same order. You can only see a rainbow when the Sun is behind you.

Rainbow after a storm in Africa

Climate in crisis

Since the last ice age, the climate on Earth has been getting warmer. In recent years, changes have happened more quickly. Because more coal and oil have been burned, the level of carbon dioxide in the atmosphere is increasing. This stops heat from escaping into space, and Earth is getting warmer. This 'greenhouse effect' is damaging our planet. We must stop polluting the atmosphere if we want to save Earth!

Acid rain

Pollution from factories mixes with water in the air and creates acid rain. This rain destroys plants, eats away at buildings and kills river fish. Acid rain is carried by wind and causes damage over a wide area.

Rising sea levels

Many scientists believe that air pollution is causing the planet's temperatures to rise. Over the next 50 years, Earth may get so much warmer that ice at the Poles will melt, and the sea levels will rise and flood the land.

Glossary

acid rain Rainwater that is full of pollution, which makes it acidic. Acid rain causes damage to trees, crops and buildings.

air pressure The weight of air on the surface of Earth, measured with a barometer.

anemometer An instrument used for measuring wind speed.

atmosphere The air that surrounds Earth. It is made up of a mixture of gases, including nitrogen, oxygen and water vapour.

climate The normal weather conditions that happen in a place over 30 years or more.

condensation The change of a gas into a liquid, such as water vapour into droplets of water.

desert An area of land where less than 25cm of rain falls every year. Deserts can either be hot or cold.

drought Long periods of time when little or no rain falls.

Equator An imaginary line round the centre of Earth.

evaporation This happens when a liquid changes into a gas – i.e. when river water, heated by the Sun's rays, becomes water vapour.

fog Water droplets in the air that make it difficult to see.

fuels Substances, such as coal, wood or petrol, that we burn to make power. Among other things, this power can be used to heat our homes.

greenhouse effect Gases such as carbon dioxide build up in the atmosphere and stop heat on Earth from escaping into space. This raises Earth's temperature and causes the 'greenhouse effect'.

high pressure When the weight of the air on Earth is high.

humid The weather is humid when the air is moist, or damp.

hurricane A violent, tropical storm that brings wind and rain. A hurricane can also be called a typhoon, or a tropical cyclone.

lightning Electricity that has built up inside a cloud and then jumps to Earth in a bright flash.

low pressure When the weight of the air on Earth is low.

meteorite A chunk of rock that crashes to Earth from space. Most are small, but some are big and can cause huge explosions.

mist Water droplets floating in the air. Mist is similar to fog but it lies closer to the ground.

monsoon A wind that blows off the sea on to the land for six months, and then blows the other way for six months.

northern hemisphere The half of Earth north of the Equator.

Poles Points at the top and bottom of Earth. The North Pole is in the Arctic region, and the South Pole is in the Antarctic region.

pollution Poisons in the environment that make us ill.

sea level The normal height of the surface of the sea.

season A period of weather lasting three or six months.

southern hemisphere The half of Earth south of the Equator.

Sun The star at the centre of our solar system, which Earth moves around, or orbits.

temperature The level of hotness of a body or substance.

thermometer An instrument that is used to measure temperature.

tornado A column of wind that spirals from the ground up to a thunder cloud. Also called a twister, or a waterspout at sea.

trade winds Winds that are always blowing over the oceans.

tropics The hot regions of the world around the Equator.

water cycle When water moves from rivers to the air and back to the land as rain.

water vapour Water in the form of a gas floating in the air.

Index